The Pond

written by Kelly Gaffney

This is a big pond.

It is in a garden.

Look into the water.

You can see little fish.

They can swim in the pond.

This is a pond, too.

You can see plants in the water.

The plants are big and green.

Look at the frog.

The frog is in the pond.

It is on a plant.

9

Look at this pond.

You can see insects in the water.

The insects are black.

They can swim in the pond.

Look at the duck.

The duck is going into a pond.

It is going for a swim.

A pond is a home for a fish.
It is a home for insects
and a frog.

A pond is a home for a duck, too.